I am Grateful for:

*
*
*
*
*

In my PRAYERS:

Always

& FOREVER

D1558445

I am...

I will...

more from my heart...

_____

_____

_____

_____

_____

date:

I am Grateful for:

※
※
※
※
※

In my PRAYERS:

RAISE A
HALLELUJAH

I am...

I will...

more from my heart...

_____
_____
_____
_____
_____

date:

I am Grateful for:

❋
❋
❋
❋
❋

That's what
FRIENDS
are for.

As iron sharpens iron, so one person sharpens another. Proverbs 27:17

In my PRAYERS:

I am...

I will...

more from my heart...

_____
_____
_____
_____
_____

date:

I am Grateful for:

✻

✻

✻

✻

✻

I sought the LORD, and he answered me;
he delivered me from all my fears.
Psalms 34:4

In my PRAYERS:

Let my faith be greater than my fear.

I am...

I will...

more from my heart...

date:

I am Grateful for:

* * * * *

Cast all your anxiety on him because he cares for you. 1 Peter 5:7

WORRY ADDS NOTHING POSITIVE TO YOUR LIFE.

I am...

more from my heart...

_____

_____

_____

_____

_____

In my PRAYERS:

I will...

date:

I am Grateful for:

＊
＊
＊
＊
＊

She who kneels before God can stand before anyone. Romans 8:31

In my PRAYERS:

THERE IS POWER IN PRAYER.

I am...

I will...

more from my heart...

_____

_____

_____

_____

_____

date:

I am Grateful for:

✳
✳
✳
✳
✳

dishes – thankful for food!
laundry – thankful for clothes!
mess – thankful for those
who made it!

> So whether you eat or drink or whatever you do, do it all for the glory of God.
> 1 Corinthians 10:31

In my PRAYERS:

I am...

I will...

more from my heart...

date:

I am Grateful for:

*
*
*
*
*

In my PRAYERS:

wired for

JOY

I am...

I will...

more from my heart...

_____

_____

_____

_____

_____

date:

I am Grateful for:

*
*
*
*
*

In my PRAYERS:

ALWAYS BE

humble & kind

I am...

I will...

more from my heart...

date:

I am Grateful for:

✳
✳
✳
✳
✳

Ask and it will be given to you;
seek and you will find;
knock and the door will be opened to you.
Matthew 7:7

In my PRAYERS:

BELIEVE **BIG**

I am...

I will...

more from my heart...

_____
_____
_____
_____
_____

date:

I am Grateful for:

✳
✳
✳
✳
✳

For we are God's handiwork, created in Christ Jesus to do good works, which God prepared in advance for us to do.
Ephesians 2:10

In my PRAYERS:

What are you created to do?

I am...

I will...

more from my heart...

date:

I am Grateful for:

✳
✳
✳
✳
✳

MY PLANS OR HIS?

When I look at the bigger picture, I want my puzzle pieces to come together as they should...not because I crammed it together!

I am...

Commit to the LORD whatever you do, and he will establish your plans.

Proverbs 16:3

In my PRAYERS:

I will...

more from my heart...

date:

I am Grateful for:

✳
✳
✳
✳
✳

Set your minds on things above, not on earthly things. Colossians 3:2

In my PRAYERS:

Feeling beaten? Only need to turn heavenward with those thoughts to find your biggest cheerleader.

I am...

I will...

more from my heart...

_____
_____
_____
_____
_____
_____

date:

I am Grateful for:

＊

＊

＊

＊

＊

Praise the LORD, my soul, and forget not all his benefits. Psalms 103:2

Let us have an

ATTITUDE *of*

GRATITUDE

In my PRAYERS:

I am...

I will...

more from my heart...

_____

_____

_____

_____

_____

date:

I am Grateful for:

✳
✳
✳
✳
✳

pray **BIG**
TRUST Him

I am...

more from my heart...

In the morning, LORD, you hear my voice;
in the morning, I lay my requests before
you & wait expectantly. Psalms 5:3

In my PRAYERS:

I will...

date:

I am Grateful for:

❋

❋

❋

❋

❋

Dear children, let us not love with words or speech but with action and in truth.

1 John 3:18

In my PRAYERS:

May all I do
show my love
for YOU!

I am...

I will...

more from my heart...

date:

I am Grateful for:

* ✳
* ✳
* ✳
* ✳
* ✳

With all my heart I praise the LORD! I will never forget how kind he has been. The LORD forgives our sins, heals us when we are sick, and protects us from death. His kindness & love are a crown on our heads. Psalms 103:2-4.

In my PRAYERS:

Kindness + Forgiveness
+ Healing
-- all from Him

I am...

I will...

more from my heart...

_____

_____

_____

_____

_____

_____

date:

I am Grateful for:

✳
✳
✳
✳
✳

Be Confident
and know that God's
mercy & grace is
abundant.

I am...

more from my heart...

_____
_____
_____
_____
_____
_____

Let us then approach God's throne of
grace with confidence, so that we may
receive mercy & find grace to help us in
our time of need. Hebrews 4:16

In my PRAYERS:

I will...

date:

I am Grateful for:

*
*
*
*
*

For I am the Lord your God who takes hold of your right hand and says to you, DO NOT FEAR; I WILL HELP YOU.

Isaiah 41:13

In my PRAYERS:

faith
fear
everyday

I am...

I will...

more from my heart...

date:

I am Grateful for:

✳
✳
✳
✳
✳

In my PRAYERS:

I'M JUST A SINNER

SAVED BY GRACE

I am...

I will...

more from my heart...

_____
_____
_____
_____
_____

date:

I am Grateful for:

＊

＊

＊

＊

＊

Listen to advice and accept discipline, and at the end you will be counted among the wise. Proverbs 19:20

In my PRAYERS:

Not my ways,
but yours!
humble & wise

I am...

I will...

more from my heart...

_____
_____
_____
_____
_____

date:

I am Grateful for:

＊

＊

＊

＊

＊

For the Spirit God gave us does not make us timid, but gives us power, love and self-discipline. 2 Timothy 1:7

In my PRAYERS:

Jesus is with me.
I can do anything.

I am...

I will...

more from my heart...

date:

I am Grateful for:

"I AM."
Exodus 3:34

※
※
※
※
※

In my PRAYERS:

SPEAK LIFE!

I AM...
BEAUTIFUL, CAPABLE,
JOYFUL, SPIRIT FILLED,
FORGIVEN, LOVING...

I am...

I will...

more from my heart...

_____
_____
_____
_____
_____

date:

I am Grateful for:

*
*
*
*
*

When the time is right, I, the Lord, will make it happen.
Isaiah 60:22

In my PRAYERS:

Trust His Timing

I am...

I will...

more from my heart...

_____
_____
_____
_____
_____

date:

I am Grateful for:

* ✳
* ✳
* ✳
* ✳
* ✳

I have died, but Christ lives in me. And now I live by faith in the Son of God, who loved me & gave his life for me. Galations 2:20

AMAZING
is his love for me!

In my PRAYERS:

I am...

I will...

more from my heart...

_____

_____

_____

_____

_____

date:

I am Grateful for:

＊

＊

＊

＊

＊

Stay joined to me & let my teachings
become part of you. Then you can pray
for whatever you want, & your prayer will
be answered. John 15:7

In my PRAYERS:

*He may not always give us
what we want but He always
gives us what we NEED.*

I am...

I will...

more from my heart...

_____

_____

_____

_____

_____

_____

date:

I am Grateful for:

*
*
*
*
*

These commandments that I give to you today are to be on your hearts. Impress them on your children. Talk about them when you sit at home & when you walk along the road, when you lie down & when you get up. Deuteronomy 6:6-7

In my PRAYERS:

24/7

I am...

I will...

more from my heart...

date:

I am Grateful for:

✳
✳
✳
✳
✳

Yet you, Lord, are our Father. We are the clay, you are the potter; we are all the work of your hand. Isaiah 64:8

In my PRAYERS:

His Masterpiece
*YOUnique * beYOUtiful*

I am...

I will...

more from my heart...

date:

I am Grateful for:

*
*
*
*
*

pause
pray
peace

Blessed are the peacemakers, for they will
be called children of God.
Matthew 5:9

In my PRAYERS:

I am...

I will...

more from my heart...

_____
_____
_____
_____
_____
_____

date:

I am Grateful for:

＊
＊
＊
＊
＊

So then, let's work for the good of all whenever we have an opportunity & especially for those in the household of faith. Galations 6:10

In my PRAYERS:

be a
HELPER, a DOER

I am...

I will...

more from my heart...

date:

I am Grateful for:

✳
✳
✳
✳
✳

It is never fun to be corrected. In fact, at the time it is always painful. But if we learn to obey by being corrected, we will do right & live at peace. Hebrews 12:11

In my PRAYERS:

learn
FROM YOUR MISTAKES

I am...

I will...

more from my heart...

date:

I am Grateful for:

✳
✳
✳
✳
✳

Then, because you belong to Christ Jesus, God will bless you with peace that no one can completely understand. And this peace will control the way you think & feel.
Philippians 4:7

In my PRAYERS:

PEACE
be with you

I am...

I will...

more from my heart...

_____
_____
_____
_____
_____
_____

date:

I am Grateful for:

✳
✳
✳
✳
✳

So then, if anyone is in Christ, that person
is part of the new creation.
The old things have gone away,
& look, new things have arrived.
2 Corinthians 5:17

In my PRAYERS:

*How amazing is new
life in Christ.*

I am...

I will...

more from my heart...

date:

I am Grateful for:

*
*
*
*
*

Submit yourselves, then, to God. Resist the devil, and he will flee from you.

James 4:7

In my PRAYERS:

Break the chains!

I am...

I will...

more from my heart...

_____
_____
_____
_____
_____

date:

I am Grateful for:

* ✳
* ✳
* ✳
* ✳
* ✳

Peace I leave with you; my peace I give you. I do not give as the world gives. Do not let your hearts be troubled & do not be afraid. John 14:27

In my PRAYERS:

Amen to the blessing of God's perfect peace.

I am...

I will...

more from my heart...

_____
_____
_____
_____
_____

date:

I am Grateful for:

✳
✳
✳
✳
✳

We can make our plans, but the Lord determines our steps. Proverbs 16:9

In my PRAYERS:

For all my planning, His plan is so much greater.

I am...

I will...

more from my heart...

_____
_____
_____
_____
_____
_____

date:

I am Grateful for:

✳
✳
✳
✳
✳

Oh, how I want to understand, but oh how I need to simply trust sometimes.

I am...

more from my heart...

_____

_____

_____

_____

_____

_____

...we ask God to give you a complete understanding of what he wants to do in your lives, & we ask him to make you wise with spiritual wisdom.
Colossians 1:9

In my PRAYERS:

I will...

date:

I am Grateful for:

❋

❋

❋

❋

❋

Do not let any unwholesome talk come out of your mouth, but only what is helpful for building others up according to their needs, that it may benefit those who listen.
Ephesians 4:29

Be Kind...
or be quiet.

In my PRAYERS:

I am...

I will...

more from my heart...

date:

I am Grateful for:

* * * * *

In my PRAYERS:

He is the perfect teacher.
...may I strive to be
an A+ student.

I am...

I will...

more from my heart...

date:

I am Grateful for:

✳
✳
✳
✳
✳

When anxiety was great within me, your consolation brought me joy. Psalms 94:19

Console me dear Lord & help me to receive your consolation -- even in my most anxious moments.

In my PRAYERS:

I am...

I will...

more from my heart...

_____
_____
_____
_____
_____

date:

I am Grateful for:

＊

＊

＊

＊

＊

Let your roots grow down into him & draw up nourishment from him, so you will grow in faith, strong & vigorous in the truth you were taught. Let your lives overflow with thanksgiving for all he has done. Colossians 2:7

In my PRAYERS:

LET ME PLANT MY FAITH FIRMLY IN THE LORD & BE THANKFUL ALWAYS.

I am...

I will...

more from my heart...

_____

_____

_____

_____

_____

date:

I am Grateful for:

❋
❋
❋
❋
❋

May each one (tribulation) strengthen my faith.

In my PRAYERS:

I am...

I will...

more from my heart...

_____
_____
_____
_____
_____

date:

I am Grateful for:

✳
✳
✳
✳
✳

In my PRAYERS:

WHERE DO YOU FIND HOPE?

I am...

I will...

more from my heart...

_____
_____
_____
_____
_____

date:

I am Grateful for:

＊

＊

＊

＊

＊

God planned for us to do good things and to live as he has always wanted us to live. This is why he sent Christ to make us what we are. Ephesians 4:10

In my PRAYERS:

God has GOOD plans for us -- really good plans...let's let Him guide us so we can enjoy them.

I am...

I will...

more from my heart...

_____

_____

_____

_____

_____

_____

date:

I am Grateful for:

✳
✳
✳
✳
✳

A loving attitude towards ALL you meet will make all the difference in your daily interactions.

Conduct yourselves with all humility, gentleness, & patience. Accept each other with love... Ephesians 4:2

In my PRAYERS:

I am...

I will...

more from my heart...

_____

_____

_____

_____

_____

date:

I am Grateful for:

✳
✳
✳
✳
✳

Every good & perfect gift comes down
from the Father who created the lights in
the heavens. He is always the same &
never makes dark shadows by changing.

James 1:17

His light through YOU is a beautiful gift!

In my PRAYERS:

I am...

I will...

more from my heart...

_____
_____
_____
_____
_____
_____

date:

I am Grateful for:

*
*
*
*
*

In my PRAYERS:

Prayer time is not optional. It's essential.

I am...

I will...

more from my heart...

_____

_____

_____

_____

_____

_____

date:

I am Grateful for:

*
*
*
*
*

In my PRAYERS:

PRAISE GOD IN
THE ORDINARY.

I am...

I will...

more from my heart...

_____

_____

_____

_____

_____

_____

date:

I am Grateful for:

✳
✳
✳
✳
✳

...but even if our bodies are breaking down on the outside, the person we are on the inside is being renewed everyday.
2 Corinthians 4:16.

THERE IS NEW LIFE EACH DAY IN HIM.

In my PRAYERS:

I am...

I will...

more from my heart...

_____

_____

_____

_____

_____

date:

I am Grateful for:

*
*
*
*
*

Hope is my Sunshine on a rainy day.

I am...

more from my heart...

_____

_____

_____

_____

_____

And the scriptures were written to teach
& encourage us by giving us hope.
Romans 15:4

In my PRAYERS:

I will...

date:

I am Grateful for:

✳
✳
✳
✳
✳

Always be joyful & never stop praying. Whatever happens, keep thanking God because of Jesus Christ. This is what God wants you to do. 1 Thessalonians 5:16-18

Be thankful in ALL circumstances.

In my PRAYERS:

I am...

I will...

more from my heart...

date:

I am Grateful for:

＊
＊
＊
＊
＊

Tell the LORD how thankful you are,
because he is kind & always merciful.
Psalms 118:1

See above! (hint: I am grateful for...his kindness, his mercy)

I am...

In my PRAYERS:

I will...

more from my heart...

date:

I am Grateful for:

❋

❋

❋

❋

❋

God is the one who makes us patient &
cheerful. I pray that he will help you live at
peace with each other as you follow
Christ. Romans 15:5

In my PRAYERS:

Daily Goal: let God help
me be patient &
cheerful

I am...

I will...

more from my heart...

_____

_____

_____

_____

_____

date:

I am Grateful for:

＊
＊
＊
＊
＊

We thank God for you & always mention you in our prayers. 1 Thessalonians 1:2

In my PRAYERS:

thankful for:
YOU

I am...

I will...

more from my heart...

_____
_____
_____
_____
_____

date:

I am Grateful for:

✳

✳

✳

✳

✳

God is the one who makes us patient & cheerful. I pray that he will help you live at peace with each other as you follow Christ. Romans 15:5

In my PRAYERS:

Daily Goal: let God help me be patient & cheerful

I am...

I will...

more from my heart...

_____

_____

_____

_____

_____

date:

I am Grateful for:

※
※
※
※
※

We thank God for you & always mention you in our prayers. 1 Thessalonians 1:2

thankful for:
YOU

In my PRAYERS:

I am...

I will...

more from my heart...

_____
_____
_____
_____
_____

date:

I am Grateful for:

✳
✳
✳
✳
✳

Neither do people light a lamp & put it under a basket. Instead they put it on top of a lampstand, & it shines on all who are in the house. Matthew 5:15

In my PRAYERS:

Be the light --
yes you!

I am...

I will...

more from my heart...

date:

I am Grateful for:

✳
✳
✳
✳
✳

We always have a safe place...with Him.

In my PRAYERS:

I am...

I will...

more from my heart...

_____
_____
_____
_____
_____

date:

I am Grateful for:

✳
✳
✳
✳
✳

Examine me, God! Look at my heart! Put me to the test! Know my anxious thoughts! Psalms 139:23

In my PRAYERS:

PRAISE MORE!
worry less!

I am...

I will...

more from my heart...

date:

I am Grateful for:

✳

✳

✳

✳

✳

Celebrate & worship his holy name with all your heart. Psalms 105:3

CELEBRATE & WORSHIP HIM!

In my PRAYERS:

I am...

I will...

more from my heart...

_____
_____
_____
_____
_____
_____

date:

I am Grateful for:

Do not be overcome by evil, but overcome evil with good. Romans 12:21

*
*
*
*
*

Go! Do!
GOOD WORKS

In my PRAYERS:

I am...

I will...

more from my heart...

_____
_____
_____
_____
_____

date:

I am Grateful for:

✳
✳
✳
✳
✳

In the same way, let your light shine before people, so they can see the good things you do & praise your Father who is in heaven. Matthew 5:16

In my PRAYERS:

Be the
GOOD

I am...

I will...

more from my heart...

_____
_____
_____
_____
_____

date:

I am Grateful for:

❋

❋

❋

❋

❋

Have mercy on me, O God, according to your unfailing love; according to your great compassion blot out my transgressions. Wash away all my iniquity and cleanse me from my sin.
Psalms 51:1-2

In my PRAYERS:

So grateful for His mercy & grace anew each day.

I am...

I will...

more from my heart...

date:

I am Grateful for:

* ✳
* ✳
* ✳
* ✳
* ✳

I keep your word close, in my heart, so that I won't sin against you. Psalms 119:11

In my PRAYERS:

I WILL CLING TO YOUR WORD

I am...

I will...

more from my heart...

date:

I am Grateful for:

✳
✳
✳
✳
✳

...among these people you SHINE like stars in the world because you hold onto the word of life... Philippians 2:15

In my PRAYERS:

SHINE
SHINE
SHINE

I am...

I will...

more from my heart...

_____
_____
_____
_____
_____
_____

date:

I am Grateful for:

※

※

※

※

※

Who will harm you if you are zealous for good? 1 Peter 3:13

In my PRAYERS:

do
GOOD

I am...

I will...

more from my heart...

_____

_____

_____

_____

_____

date:

I am Grateful for:

❄
❄
❄
❄
❄

The eyes of the Lord watch over those who do right, & his ears are open to their prayers. 1 Peter 3:12

In my PRAYERS:

HEAR MY PRAYER
O LORD

I am...

I will...

more from my heart...

_____
_____
_____
_____
_____

date:

I am Grateful for:

✳
✳
✳
✳
✳

It is God who arms me with strength and
keeps my way secure. 2 Samuel 22:33

In my PRAYERS:

LEAN
ON HIM

I am...

I will...

more from my heart...

_____
_____
_____
_____
_____

date:

I am Grateful for:

He will yet fill your mouth with laughter and your lips with shouts of joy. Job 8:21

*

*

*

*

*

fill me with laughter & joy so much it's contagious

In my PRAYERS:

I am...

I will...

more from my heart...

_____

_____

_____

_____

_____

date:

I am Grateful for:

✳
✳
✳
✳
✳

Rich and poor have this in common:
The Lord is the Maker of them all.
Proverbs 22:2

In my PRAYERS:

We are ALL
children of God,
sisters & brothers.

I am...

I will...

more from my heart...

_____
_____
_____
_____
_____
_____

date:

I am Grateful for:

*
*
*
*
*

Each one of you is part of the body of Christ, and you were chosen to live together in peace. So let the peace that comes from Christ control your thoughts. And be grateful. Colossians 3:15

In my PRAYERS:

Let go...
Give Him control

I am...

I will...

more from my heart...

_____
_____
_____
_____
_____
_____

date:

I am Grateful for:

＊

＊

＊

＊

＊

Therefore, stop worrying about tomorrow because tomorrow will worry about itself. Each day has enough trouble of its own.

Matthew 6:34

In my PRAYERS:

turn your worry into prayer

I am...

I will...

more from my heart...

date:

I am Grateful for:

❋

❋

❋

❋

❋

Whatever you have learned or received or heard from me or seen in me, put it into practice & the God of peace will be with you. Philippians 4:9

God's peace is yours to receive.

In my PRAYERS:

I am...

I will...

more from my heart...

_____

_____

_____

_____

_____

date:

I am Grateful for:

✳
✳
✳
✳
✳

If you are having trouble, you should pray. And if you are feeling good, you should sing praises. James 5:13

In my PRAYERS:

Prayer
& PRAISE

I am...

I will...

more from my heart...

date:

I am Grateful for:

＊
＊
＊
＊
＊

I am the Lord, the God of ALL mankind. Is anything to hard for me? Jeremiah 32:27

In my PRAYERS:

NOTHING IS IMPOSSIBLE
FOR GOD.

I am...

I will...

more from my heart...

date:

I am Grateful for:

﹡

﹡

﹡

﹡

﹡

We do not want you to become lazy, but to imitate those who through faith and patience inherit what has been promised.

Hebrews 6:12

PUT YOUR FAITH IN ACTION

In my PRAYERS:

I am...

I will...

more from my heart...

_____

_____

_____

_____

_____

date:

I am Grateful for:

＊
＊
＊
＊
＊

Do not merely listen to the word, and so deceive yourselves. Do what it says.
James 1:22

In my PRAYERS:

#godogoodWorks

I am...

I will...

more from my heart...

date:

I am Grateful for:

✳
✳
✳
✳
✳

"He himself bore our sins" in his body on the cross, so that we might die to sins and live for righteousness; "by his wounds you have been healed." 1 Peter 2:24

In my PRAYERS:

...by His wounds you have been healed

I am...

I will...

more from my heart...

_____
_____
_____
_____
_____
_____

date:

I am Grateful for:

＊
＊
＊
＊
＊

For I know the plans I have for you, declares the Lord, plans to prosper you and not to harm you, plans to give you hope and a future. Jeremiah 29:11

In my PRAYERS:

Trust His Plan

I am...

I will...

more from my heart...

_____

_____

_____

_____

_____

date:

I am Grateful for:

✳
✳
✳
✳
✳

UNSWERVING
Faith

In my PRAYERS:

I am...

I will...

more from my heart...

date:

I am Grateful for:

✳
✳
✳
✳
✳

Don't be like the people of this world, but let God change the way you think. Then you will know how to do everything that is good & pleasing to him. Romans 12:2

In my PRAYERS:

Don't have a wordly view.

Have a Godly view.

I am...

I will...

more from my heart...

_____
_____
_____
_____
_____
_____

date:

I am Grateful for:

✳
✳
✳
✳
✳

We should keep on encouraging each other to be thoughtful & to do helpful things. Hebrews 10:24

In my PRAYERS:

Do Good.
BE KIND.

I am...

I will...

more from my heart...

_____
_____
_____
_____
_____
_____

date:

I am Grateful for:

※
※
※
※
※

In my PRAYERS:

*Trust & obey,
for there's no
other way.*

I am...

I will...

more from my heart...

_____

_____

_____

_____

_____

date:

I am Grateful for:

Don't let evil conquer you, but conquer
evil by doing good. Romans 12:21

*

*

*

*

*

In my PRAYERS:

FIGHT EVIL
WITH GOODNESS.

I am...

I will...

more from my heart...

date:

I am Grateful for:

❋
❋
❋
❋
❋

With all your heart you must trust the Lord & not your own judgement.
Proverbs 3:5

In my PRAYERS:

TRUST
Him

I am...

I will...

more from my heart...

_____

_____

_____

_____

_____

date:

I am Grateful for:

✳
✳
✳
✳
✳

Shine so that others see Him in you.

So our faces are not covered. They show the bright glory of the Lord, as the Lord's Spirit makes us more & more like our glorious Lord. 2 Corinthians 3:18

In my PRAYERS:

I am...

I will...

more from my heart...

_____
_____
_____
_____
_____

date:

I am Grateful for:

✳
✳
✳
✳
✳

Yes, my soul, find rest in God; my hope comes from him. Psalms 62:5

In my PRAYERS:

NEVER GIVE UP HOPE

I am...

I will...

more from my heart...

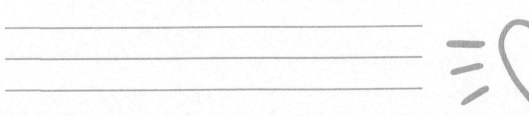

date:

I am Grateful for:

If you are cheerful, you feel good; if you are sad, you hurt all over. Proverbs 17:22

✳
✳
✳
✳
✳

In my PRAYERS:

Choose to be cheerful

I am...

I will...

more from my heart...

_____
_____
_____
_____
_____
_____

date:

I am Grateful for:

✳
✳
✳
✳
✳

Certainly the faithful love of the LORD
hasn't ended; certainly God's compassion
isn't through! Lamentations 3:22

He is faithful &
compassionate
always.

In my PRAYERS:

I am...

I will...

more from my heart...

_____
_____
_____
_____
_____

date:

I am Grateful for:

✳
✳
✳
✳
✳

Generous persons will prosper; those who refresh others will themselves be refreshed. Proverbs 11:25

In my PRAYERS:

be a GIVER

I am...

I will...

more from my heart...

_____
_____
_____
_____
_____
_____

date:

I am Grateful for:

*
*
*
*
*

Friends love all the time, & kinsfolk are born for times of trouble. Proverbs 17:17

In my PRAYERS:

Friends are your chosen family.

I am...

I will...

more from my heart...

_____

_____

_____

_____

_____

date:

I am Grateful for:

✳
✳
✳
✳
✳

Pursue the LORD and his strength; seek his face always! 1 Chronicles 16:11

In my PRAYERS:

SEEK & you
will FIND.

I am...

I will...

more from my heart...

date:

I am Grateful for:

*

*

*

*

*

If you are angry, you cannot do any of the good things God wants done. James 1:20

In my PRAYERS:

#choosehappy

I am...

I will...

more from my heart...

_____

_____

_____

_____

_____

_____

date:

I am Grateful for:

*
*
*
*
*

In my PRAYERS:

GIVE
THANKS

I am...

I will...

more from my heart...

date:

I am Grateful for:

※
※
※
※
※

You are my shelter & my shield -- I wait for your promise. Psalms 119:114

His promises are good!

In my PRAYERS:

I am...

I will...

more from my heart...

_____
_____
_____
_____
_____

date:

I am Grateful for:

✳
✳
✳
✳
✳

In my PRAYERS:

Seek & you will find!

I am...

I will...

more from my heart...

_____

_____

_____

_____

_____

date:

I am Grateful for:

✳
✳
✳
✳
✳

Does not wisdom call out? Does not understanding raise her voice? At the highest point along the way, where the paths meet, she takes her stand;
Proverbs 8:1-2

In my PRAYERS:

Seek
WISDOM

I am...

I will...

more from my heart...

_____
_____
_____
_____
_____

date:

I am Grateful for:

✳
✳
✳
✳
✳

But it is the spirit in a person, the breath of the Almighty, that gives them understanding. Job 32:8

In my PRAYERS:

Spirit
Fill me!

I am...

I will...

more from my heart...

_____
_____
_____
_____
_____

date:

I am Grateful for:

✳
✳
✳
✳
✳

You are saved by God's grace because of your faith. This salvation is God's gift. It's not something you possessed.

Ephesians 2:8

In my PRAYERS:

Amazing
Grace

I am...

I will...

more from my heart...

_____

_____

_____

_____

_____

_____

date:

I am Grateful for:

＊
＊
＊
＊
＊

Blessed
to be a
blessing

I am...

In my PRAYERS:

I will...

more from my heart...

_____
_____
_____
_____
_____
_____

date:

I am Grateful for:

✳
✳
✳
✳
✳

I will praise the LORD who counsels me --
even at night my conscience instructs me.

Psalms 16:7

He is the mighty counselor.

In my PRAYERS:

I am...

I will...

more from my heart...

_____
_____
_____
_____
_____

date:

I am Grateful for:

*
*
*
*
*

Glory to God!

In my PRAYERS:

I am...

I will...

more from my heart...

_____

_____

_____

_____

_____

date:

Made in the USA
Middletown, DE
19 December 2020